T0304551

more praise for
WINTER WORK

"There is maturity in these poems. Sit down with him in a wild place and listen. He knows."

LANCE HENSON
Cheyenne Dog Soldier

"These poems offer clear, clean witnessing of our beautiful, aching world. Here 'in the shadow of the tower' of the California Missions, with death as ongoing companion, Meadows brings us into deep sensory presence, filling us with reverence for each living moment, with grief for each precious, passing being."

KITTY COSTELLO
author of *Upon Waking*
and cofounder of the TallMountain Circle

Stephen Meadow's latest collection of poems is just that, poems. His work escapes categorization other than that of poetry. You hear the poems from the page; you smell the flowers, wooded places, meadows, and the ancestors he speaks of. You feel the river flow. The poems touch a place where poetry arrives in both strength and beauty.

LINDA NOEL
Poet Laureate of Ukiah Emerita

NOMADIC PRESS

OAKLAND

PHILADELPHIA

XALAPA

WWW.NOMADICPRESS.ORG

MASTHEAD

FOUNDING PUBLISHER
J. K. Fowler

ASSOCIATE EDITOR
Michaela Mullin

LEAD EDITOR
Kim Shuck

DESIGN
Jevohn Tyler Newsome

MISSON STATEMENT Through publications, events, and active community participation, Nomadic Press collectively weaves together platforms for intentionally marginalized voices to take their rightful place within the world of the written and spoken word. Through our limited means, we are simply attempting to help right the centuries' old violence and silencing that should never have occurred in the first place and build alliances and community partnerships with others who share a collective vision for a future far better than today.

INVITATIONS Nomadic Press wholeheartedly accepts invitations to read your work during our open reading period every year. To learn more or to extend an invitation, please visit: www.nomadicpress.org/invitations

DISTRIBUTION
Orders by teachers, libraries, trade bookstores, or wholesalers:

Nomadic Press Distribution
orders@nomadicpress.org
(510) 500-5162

Small Press Distribution
spd@spdbooks.org
(510) 524-1668 / (800) 869-7553

Winter Work

This book was made possible by a loving community of chosen family and friends, old and new.

For author questions or to book a reading at your bookstore, university/school, or alternative establishment, please send an email to info@nomadicpress.org.

Cover art: Kim Shuck (photo by Doug Salin)

Artist portrait by Arthur Johnstone

Published by Nomadic Press, 1941 Jackson Street, Suite 20, Oakland, CA 94612

First printing, 2022

Library of Congress Cataloging-in-Publication Data

Title: ***Winter Work***
p. cm.

Summary: Stephen Meadows' *Winter Work* is a collection that resounds with intense observations of place. Each poem is a clean and reverent gesture of understanding–natural elements, the damage we inflict upon the land, our history. With brevity and precision, he takes readers on a journey of illness, grief, love, and quiet joy. Memories make story and Meadows makes the geography of feeling a map of locations we want to explore.

[1. POETRY / American / Native American. 2. POETRY / Subjects & Themes / Nature. 3. POETRY / Subjects & Themes / Places. 4. POETRY / American / General.]

LIBRARY OF CONGRESS CONTROL NUMBER: 2022944121

ISBN: 978-1-955239-33-2

WINTER WORK

WINTER WORK

POEMS BY

STEPHEN
MEADOWS

NOMADIC PRESS

Oakland · Philadelphia · Xalapa

CONTENTS

foreword by Kim Shuck
introduction

notes
reading guide

.

FOREWORD

It may be that the first time I read Stephen Meadows' work it was on a bronze plaque on San Francisco's Embarcadero. It may be that we were thrown together in a poetry reading because we are both from First Peoples and that is often how I meet other Indigenous poets. The truth is that although I've been trying to remember the first time I read Stephen, I can't. I can say that his stripped, deep gazing poems bring me back over and over. He was one of the handful of poets that I read during my inaugural speech as Poet Laureate of San Francisco. I carried his first book of poems around with me for years. I'm a big fan.

"White trunks of birches
dismember the darkness"

Once dismembered how do we reassemble ourselves, our place, our cultures?

Poetry is an art of self, a sculpture in words that we make of the experience our own bodies, our own perceptions. It's a very intimate art. Meadows' writing speaks to human distance from and resonance with our knowing of one another, of our places. Every poem is couched in a relentless precision of the senses. This absolute gaze settles the "I" of the poem deeply into the moment. At the same time, the clarity, the utterly un-baffled clarity, of the images takes the "I" out of the tumble and fret of living. The images are beautiful, and unsentimental.

"... you cannot but witness
looking out from that bleak place"

What does standing as witness cost in songs like these?

There is nothing static about these poems. The storms, the fog, the rain, the snow, there is movement in Stephen's poems. This place may be bleak, but it is not forever. The thoughts and experiences are being digested, processed slowly. The mountains process the water. The trees are vertical streams, throwing their own wealth of chemistry. All of this quiet and deep working, this careful building of fires and shelters and connections, this is a slow healing. These poems know California. They know death and scar and weather and at the heart of it all they know the growing that takes the time to build and spill.

"night close
in the pines
about the windows
life waiting
just ahead"

How close can you let the night get?

Winter Work is an act of regrouping, perhaps of evaluation. Life power is gone deep and resting. There is a pause between the breaths between actions. We are here in the aftermath of something, something weighty but we can only see the event in as effect rather than action. The poet remains: drives nails, visits memories, visits friends, scans the tree line. These poems are a deep stock-taking, a forensic examination of a life as the scene of the disruption. In winter we examine our shadows, and there are shadows in these poems, facts in these poems. There is a deep knowing that can only come from an interior silence. Somehow, even though poems are made of words, the silence comes through.

"Sun and slow shadow
snake and rock silence"

What will you find in the slow shadows?

KIM SHUCK

7th San Francisco Poet Laureate
and author of *Deer Trails*

INTRODUCTION

I was 14 or so when I started writing, and have been writing poetry ever since. I've found it to be one of the most beautiful ways to communicate with people. My writing is a direct expression of how I feel about my experience in the world. I tend to reflect everything off nature because I find myself in sync with the pulse of the world around me, especially in its natural state. I prefer mirroring the natural world as best I can through my own consciousness. I think this is very much how Indigenous people see the world; even if they live in cities, they see the nature that was there before the city.

I write poems because I can't not write poems. I'm hoping my work will lead you to see in the writing things I didn't intentionally place there. I like to think of my work as the cleanest vision I can present. These poems are the least cluttered versions of the world, as I experience it, and I am attempting to present a complex picture from various points.

All my poems are written out longhand and then transcribed into type. This is part of the editorial process, as well. I adjust them until they are finished, and when they are typed, they are the way I want them. It's a very manual process. I think this value is reflected in the writing—the things that I am doing in the poems are very physical.

I'm more curious about your takeaway than I am in telling you how to react. This is the finest work I can do, the pinnacle of my achievement as a poet. I hope you enjoy them.

STEPHEN MEADOWS

ON THE ROAD BEFORE RAIN

Over towards Coquille
I watch the rain come
the bruise of it softening
the jagged logged ridge
From this barn roof
banging down the wide nails
a foot at a time
no one sees cleaner
the quick track of this storm
chasing the blue stone road
upriver to the peaks
the farmhouse away near the creek
now swallowed by weather
its chimney smoke scattered
in the moments just before
the first cold waves of mist
bury the barn

VIRGINIA CHRISTMAS

Hot smoke in the lungs
one cigarette after another
lit lying down
under corrugated iron
behind the pumps
of the busted gas house
outside of Roanoke
Freezing rain pounds
on the cold tin roofing
sheets of hail seethe
in the flash
of bolt lightning
soaked boots
and frozen jeans
broke and no hope
left for Christmas
with friends
matches and smoke
sealed tight in the pocket
of the third coat in
from the ground

THEMSELVES
EACH ONE

Columns of rain cloud
stacked against the ridge
acacia in full bloom
wet over the cemetery road
It is true that rocks move
in the soil
these gravestones are new
emerging last night
like blooms that surprise
after weeks of watching them swell
the names and numbers as clear
as when metal bit stone
The mourners and close friends
leaving in clusters through the years
walking by this yard full of bones
themselves each one not believing
in a nameless rest

AFTER THE FACT

The Quake of '89

Flashlights twitch
along the ruined main street
in the rubble flesh stiffens
while red lights strobe
above the heads of those living
after the fact
From the raw dark
a woman's voice wails
unashamed
shards of glass tinkling
like macabre chimes
embodying the wind
New shocks juggle the debris
of this tremor
that renders the fault even
by dismembering
all the years

AIRBORNE

Water poured down
on the death house roof
filled the gutters
and low spots
to the ankle outside
In the casket
your lips shut forever
as if they'd been stapled
no one mentioned the needle
though the minister said
you won two bronze stars
in the sky over Vietnam
and said you were jubilant
and kind
The way you'd look at me
stoned
pronounce my name slow
with a reverence
through the drugs
and the beer
Your friends were all there
your tiny child clinging
while we slowly filed by
to a quiet woman
stoic in the rain

WE ARE YET INNOCENT

No time have I spent
at your grave
but your grave visits me
in my loft at night
the birds quiet
in the trees
and the damp wind
fingering the house
your face in that coffin
before you went down
not at rest
or at peace
interrupted mid thought
that absolved look
that says I know more
than I am saying
I know more

THE DOE

Cresting the ridge
at dawn
in the dark
the engine of the
forty-six pickup
the lights
on the road
she dives out of the brush
in my headlights
is blind
quivering in the dust
she cannot believe
her death
as men with knives
lead her into the trees

THE NUANCES
OF GRIEF

It has come to this shared room
in a cheap stucco rest home
your last thirty days
on our hearts
like betrayal's cold silver
By your bedside in darkness
a firmament of losses
the photos of children
glow soft by the night light
that watches you sleep out
the nightmarish violence
whatever phantasms
derangement has ordered
whatever sad memories you're allowed
In your small bed suspended
you stare through the shadows
in a rare lucid moment
pick lint from your blanket
conversing with no one
your mouth a small pocket of
woolen words
imprisoning the sound

THE OTHERS

Skewed against a window
he converses with himself
his bent shape resembling
his chair's steel wheels

With the cruelest of effort
he pronounces each word
his face twisting syllables
into a rude form of speech

In the crowded room others
pretend not to notice
look beyond out the window
where the wind bends the trees

LEAVING THE HOSPITAL

The tubes in your arm
of no use to memory
the off-white room
full of bedding and linoleum
the view from the window
in this junkyard of bodies
pristine onto pine woods
beyond the parked cars

Your breathing comes hard
as if miles sloped away
beneath your sleep
the life
with each cramped breath
lingers then goes
into the still pale moment
beyond recall

AT TWILIGHT

Nodding in your favorite chair
gone home to your childhood
your swollen hands rigid
in the arthritic stillness
you once held in tight fists
my future
I am your disappointment
I know all the secrets
you have never relinquished
though now it is all you can manage
to remember your name

FOR CHIEF JOSEPH

Your cook fires here
just a short time ago
you passed without sound
by this stream in the dark
the smoke now in tatters
in the dawn wind unfurling
like the death
in bad blankets
of your merciful wisdom
the blue world you worshiped
now follows you solemn
as a grave

ON TRIGO STREET

Squatting in the alley
baking smoked colored bread
around a five-gallon pickle
tin stove our clothes homemade
we gleaned what we needed
from the street
our anguished conversation
and a need to be new
I can never forget
how you cried that night
when we tried to make love
fully clothed and ashamed
because you'd been raped
as a child just twelve
and I had never made love at all

TODOS SANTOS

She lives twenty miles
from the nearest small village
along a road not traveled
but by trucks taking men to work
The wind is a butcher
carving up the mesquite
blowing this way every day
as the evening comes down
the layered raincloud
over the mountains
now rose
now bruise colored
Her clothes no better
than those of one who has spent
what remains of a life
on the curb of some street
she holds her child close
looking seaward to the wind
the long dress billowing behind her
the child sleeping quiet
in her arms
It blows this way each day
unforgiving from the west
though she smiles

as if the small hut beside her
made of rough sacks and tin
could deliver up Christ

ROSEBURG

From a ridge through
Oregon mist the incessant
snag and fart of the saws

A gang of tin hats
comes out black faced
shouldering chain and gas
from a down-to-dark cut

chill alder yellowing
in the blue smoke
of trucks going home

IN THE WOODS NEAR COOS BAY

Along the slung gravel track
the split shake cabins of
loggers steam between rains
the sun in jewels among
the branches of the fir trees
left to border this road
In the distance the wrack
of a big chain blade
that ever-present sound
in these gorgeous lost woods
and the wet rush
the hurtle of chip trucks
on route 42

THE INTRUSION

The furred hood of morning
crowds close about the house
Down the canyon it is silent
as time before sound
White trunks of birches
dismember the darkness
from streambed to cabin
In this belljar of woodland
the snow moving in from the brushline
waits cold at the door

IN THE SHADOW OF THE TOWER

In the quiet
your photo is upon me
you are fond of this setting
the mission adobe
where they murdered our people
in the name of a merciful god
It is history you tell me
your daughter now drinks
from the same cup
takes names from their water
You have taken their story
as your own
You have lived their religion
Your children grow up
in the shadow of the tower
where the bells of the fathers
rang bodies into the fields
In your eyes in the photo
that sadness gapes open
like the mouths of those
dead ones you cannot but witness
looking out from that bleak place
unknowing and imprisoned in the dark

A FIRE IF IT BURNS

Bent willows rattle
in the wind overhead
The remnant of the match
still smokes in your hand
I was twelve you were fifty
I was fifty you were twelve
Hovered over the wet wood
that barely burning symbol
of the generations passing
In the thicket near
that rumble of the river
your eyes red as firelight
from drinking all the beers
The white man's curse upon each
swimming that rare blood
With the roar of the wind
and water in the trees
you stared across that fifty
years the wild eyes rough
as the stubble of your jaw
the despair planted then
on the full of drift river
comes home every Christmas
everlasting
like that other kind of gift

STILL A PART OF THAT FREEDOM

Raking up these leaves
I thought of you thinking
of Paris and why you planted
these trees
The brown pointed hands
pinwheeling through the air
across the yard in the changeable
wind I remember your stories of a sergeant
driving a truck in the army
just after liberation
how the plane tree confetti
tied you there to that pavement
where the people just glad
to be alive lined the curbs
with their bodies
so for once you
belonged

THE ARTIST

for Mark Wagner

Fingers spread wide
against the limestone wall
He blows red dust
over a rough hand
leaving a new mark
The dark sack of night
down cold over the snowfields
fire licking the edges
of an orange pit
filling a black room

AS IF GOD
WERE THERE

You were my crutch then
I held to your body
for the few simple moments it took
your expressionless face
I'll choose the word mask
as you chose to use crutch
as your metaphor for love-
somewhere else but below me
in the wondrous half-light of your room
your face betrayed nothing
your crutch against your lack of faith
as I strained in your body
for approval
that numb disenchantment
in your eyes
that would not see mine
but only stared at the ordinary ceiling
as if God were there

MY MOTHER TOLD ME

for Alex Ramirez

Listen to the story

It is the wind
talking

In the pine boughs
above us
it is whispering

If you listen
you can hear

Without it
this story
in the blue air
We are lost
to one another
We are strangers
to our selves

In the pines here
the wind is talking
The words will keep us
safe and one people
together
on this bright edge
of worlds

FIREWOOD I

Driving a wedge
through a persistent rain
the mud and wet dust
splatters out with each blow
the ring of the tempered
steel arouses the dogs
the barking and the seeming chimes
in the soaking forest
end
when that final heave
clefts the giant round
the sound now
of water platting
the porch boards
the sweat wiped
I bend slow
to free up tools
and the new log ready
for fire

UNDER THE BRANCHES

When I broke down
my skull filled
with noise
the sound of
a freeway
at five o'clock
not only the sound of it
but the real
danger there
the street
so quiet
in December
the hospital ahead
the gray cold
granite
and the crushed leaves

FIREWOOD II

Smoke hugs the
hollows the
burn piles
these logged over
canyons
My boots crush
the silence
breaking up
crusted ice
I am hunting
manzanita
Lean bones of this
hard wood
make the hottest
of fires
At sundown
the memory not lost
picking up
scattered limbs
like those ones
before me
I am living
fists tight
upon the song

ABOVE THE AMERICAN

On a red dirt road
climbing the grade
into pines
Cloud on the ridges
in the higher Sierra
Below in black oak
a cold twist
of the river
Sun and slow shadow
Snake and rock silence
The stark slanted peace
of the canyon

IN SILENCE

My punishment
settled in slowly
I had thought
you might write
What was not said
has come with the rains
the hills berry colored
and fragrant
below the north ridge

AFTER LOVE

Here in a warm loft
the whimsical touch
of your nails
on my spine after love
your hands about the nerves
of my various souls
your fingers at play
in the small of my back
where the sweat pools
unmindful of losses
outside in the garden
the wind takes the leaves
from their wristed places
in the trees
building quiet on the soil

ALONE

The storm
has been blowing all night
There are no lights
for miles
The roof nearly blown
off the stable in the dark
the horses soaking
patient in the wind
I am pleased
with the quiet
with this isolating weather
with the simple heat
leaking from a woodstove
out of the rain

THE PLOW AND THE STARS

I work alone
in the greenish light
hand on the lever
that moves my blade
The quiet flakes
pour down through the beams
that probe a thin
column of this storm
In a darkened cab
only the eight hour night
spent shifting whiteness
into heaps here and there
From this mountain
the far city twinkles below
all thought here relinquished
given over to silence
and the snow

SNOW NEARING ELKO

The belly of the valley
into jubilant distance
cold crested ranges
becalmed by these flakes
up ahead the horizon
the stained Ruby Mountains
the sagebrush the gone trees
the stark flanks of foothills
the winded last light
and this pinwheeling whiteness
this freedom
overtaken by the dark

RESILIENCE

Up here
the long wind
the chaste clouds
the storming

A lean heart
on a gray ridge
snows
on the move
at morning

FROM A HOTEL IN ELKO

Four stories below
a drunk
hands raised
gropes blind
for the bar door
closed
Some black birds
stuck to frozen lines
neon signs for poker/slots
snow on the mountains
asphalt ice
rusted trucks in white
chill light
on broken streets
it's April and still
no spring

WHERE ONE BIRD CALLS

I find myself waiting
for the rain
Across the valley
clouds close with the ridge
the air not yet fluid
but taut about the cabin
and fence line
where one bird calls

CONFIDENCES

for Terry

Point Lobos
and the lost coast
beckoning like fire
We sat
each staring
at a green
lighted clock
in the dash
of that car
years ago
In that silence
the fog made
my words
matter less
than the act
of your listening
and your hearing
what I said
Night close
in the pines
about the windows
life waiting
just ahead

IMAGE AND DARKNESS

On the dull edge
of springtime
white fields stand
and shudder
this snow
and new grasses
intermingled
in the cold
words emerge slowly
in a small fire's
language
the halting tight
stutter of image
and darkness
with the light

FAITH

A cold hill
the leaves down
pine needles
drop
disconsolate
destitute
brown
In the news
all day world
economies fall
more talk
of another
depression
I sit here
quiet
in late
middle age
across the field
a woodpecker
raps
behind me
the moon
climbs out
of the pines

pulling in
the last
of the light

AT THE CROSSING

A chainsaw dismembers the silence
of a white afternoon

in a pasture
the crackle of fires
in a pruned orchard wood

little to do midwinter
but cut and burn trash

drink warm booze
in long sleeves

and watch the smoke
crossing the river
enter in among the trees

NEVADA

Out here the bruised mountains
and a sun falling fast
just the sound
of those trucks
on the highway
these yellow leaves
sheltering
and the moon
a frail disc that is risen
half a purple world away

APPROACHING SPRING

Jays call
one another
through clean
winter light
cats roll
in wet leaves
amid piles
of horse dung
no work
and no poems
the sun
warm enough
to afford
even the failed
among us
pleasure

THESE MOUNTAINS

for Dave Dalton

These mountains
are all we have left
sons and daughters
these leaves in the wind
that call us
these limbs and these
branches that enfold us
these fortresses of the soul

It is all we have left
these clouds
upon the ridges
these storms upon the morning
and the light
from the sundown
cast red over the hills

If we lose all of this
we are gone
sons and daughters
If we care now so little
no doctor
no lawyer
no shaman in the world

can ever rekindle
our spirits
our lives
this solace
this soft shade
this living green wind
among the trees

UNRECKONED

For a small voice
I feel everlasting
the lupines and poppies
erupting
the black oaks in
vibrance
all grasses
the bird and the
insects
the hawk
combing hillsides
the piles of cloud
east on the mountains
loosing high Sierra snow

Unreckoned
in this meadow
my shadow
my presence
these words
becoming less
than the tiniest
of breezes in the
quiet grey pines

over the hill
I am here
none the less
and I feel like
I have lasted
for all time
I have survived

THE DYING PLACE

You are herded
to a meal
you've forgotten
how to swallow

The white caps
of nurses
are curt
among the wheelchairs

The grey heads
are tilted like blossoms
in a memory garden
each to its own sun

CLEAR CUT

Black faced
in the smoke
Camel bent
on your lip
You are back
from dead
once more
when I walk
these hills
Your rat bit
truck hub deep
in red dust
tin hat
hooked up
behind one ear
old rope
and thirty aught
six
in the rack
crushed bed full
of odd chain
and those saws
trees all around
laid waste

in the cut
slash fires
burning
all the rest

BEYOND THE FENCES

Cut off from the rest of it
with only the heat
of the woodstove
and the birds waking
the valley at dawn
the lines of blooming
acacia on the ridge
a yellow not found
in any painting grins
quietly waiting
above the tombstones
of the graveyard
the dew on the wild
grasses falling the few inches
to earth as the sun
warms the horses
and the dogs barking
out beyond the fences
oblivious and shrill

THE GARDEN

In these mountains
of root and rock
my shovel interjects
small niches
underneath
these trees

This spading done
over and over
year after year
dislodges
disarrays
interrupting
the natural abandon
just enough
that the sun
climbing steady
through branches
provides a few
small tomatoes
a disconsolate
gourd

BONNEVILLE

Mountains float
the salt lakes
rafts on the mirage

Across the flats
a long train
the red steel
just ahead of the storm

Clouds roil black behind
bearing down
engine wise

Before the snow
shafts of sleet
the wind
the disconsolate brine

FOR KATE WOLF

The lid of that last night
closes over the land
Crickets in the dark brush
symphonize the wind
Still youthful
the singer lies dying
in a small pastel room
She can hear the cool fog
in the chorus of insects
the luminous vault of the sea mist
Imprisoning the sound

BLACK LUNG

Hellward
in cages
in tunnels
full of dust
drilling and
blasting
a billion years back
in absolute darkness
a quarter mile down
the miner now 60
feels the hardness
of anthracite
settle
in the coffins
of his lungs
that pressure
bearing away
each breath
like eons
on the coal

NEAR THE HOT SPRINGS AT MONO

The clear air
is dancing
over jade colored
snowmelt
The gray stone
has faces
implacable
and stark
On this lake
in this fastness
there is a quiet above all
The gorge leading out
of this glacial place
gleams
The clattering river
is so far below us
all we can hear
is the sun

WARREN STREET

Out the window
white roses
waves pop
the beach sand
In the bay
under darkness
a lone buoy clangs
the smell of fish
slime drift
gathering in the rocks
a squint-eyed moon
in trees
beyond the trestle

THE CLEARING

Crickets once again
in the night outside
a sound like rushes
on the surface
of the air
a not quite monotonous
jazz
an incantatory
churning
On the edge
of this clearing
fog bending
over the house
the olive trees
silver
over the ground
wings among grasses
surrounding and conscious
in darkness
at the doorway
to dreams

UP ON THE ROOF

Leaves unique
as snowflakes are
click in the wind
and pinwheel down
to red earth
through yellow air

Here the quick space
of just a second
sees a thousand
twist and fall

My gutters
scraped out yesterday
with a bloody hand
are full of them
again

IN THE BOTTOMS

Down in the willows
the sound of a saxophone
meanders on a slight wind
up across the fields
the tentative sad notes blown
slowly over water
a blues that hits home
this night with you away
the country all around
bereft of reasons
and of thought
my own sense sifted
through that blue sax
under the black skies

EUCALYPTUS

Torn orange bark
limbs littering
the road
We walk
the boy asking
about the trees
their medicinal
smell
I tell him
of past days
when I slept
in old trucks
and the groves
sent me down
enough branches
for a fire
every night

DAWN

Lantern glow
on redwood
in the dark
outside
the slightest wind
in the leaves
the tiniest
change
in night
small birds
from hidden
places
hold
then let go
one by one
the language
of light

DROUGHT

Hot breath
on lupine
on sizzling
Sierra
parched grass
the seed pods
tick soft
in slow wind
on the skittle
this summer
madrones
are bright
yellow
ponderosa
brown needles
low water
sucks
the stone

TO WINTER

Night dives
like an owl
the brown river
rises
he tends
the sad fire
a kind of
victory
in the rain
he mutters
placing
broken sticks
in homage
to this winter
where all
comes down
about him
dark
and storm

CREATION

Through an opaque green screen of honeysuckle leaves
the rain breeze as April is diminished
across the valley under the dingy quilt
of the storm the high whine of the wells
in the riverbed bringing up water
the benches of new grass the columns of alder
the quickening pace of the wind the last of winter
my place chosen well
a door at either end one east
one west to catch the last of the sun
the woodstove cast in Seattle in 1900
and water in the pipes I have lived here now
three years and my gardens all thrive
the roses of Sutter the sweet coals golden
perfuming the rank horse dung
the jasmine and suckle flower soothing
the slats of this shack
the poems like this one made slowly
as the leaves crawl out from the limbs of these vines

the slow words edging from the left
where before nothing lived

READING GUIDE

Some poems ask questions that can be answered and some poems ask questions that need to be asked over and over, with the knowledge that they will always have a different answer.

Stephen Meadows' poems continually realign self, in relationship to weather, to plants, to animals. Although nature is a common theme in poetry it is often nature in service to the human, this is not the case in Meadows' poems:

> *If there is a storm, what is it doing?*
> *If there is rain, how is one trying to stay dry?*

This relationship is not one of human control over anything non-human, but it is one of acceptance and engagement. The structure of these poems has a similar underlying idea:

> *How little can the writer describe and still present a complete and relatable image?*

Relationships with the Non-Human World

Our relationships with non-human elements in our environments often grow from our cultural stories. These stories tend to determine how we value rocks, water, weather, plants, and animals. Stephen Meadows' work reflects a specific way of valuing and gaining insight from natural objects, beings, and phenomena. This section of *Winter Work* is meant to encourage readers and students to investigate the world view represented in these poems and to write their own pieces that explore personal relationships to the things around them.

How do you react to weather?

- Describe the moment in the day when you notice the weather. Can you see or hear the weather as you wake up or are you more isolated from it?
    - Is it something that you seek out or is it something that happens to you?

- Describe a moment of being indoors with a raging storm outside.
    - How does that make you feel?

- Have you ever slept outside in the rain? Walked in the rain on purpose?
    - What words come to mind about that experience?

- Does different weather make you feel more or less connected to the world around you?

What kinds of trees mean things to you?

- Was there a tree near your home that you looked at when you were in a certain mood?
    - o Describe that mood.
- What do falling leaves mean to you?
    - o Beyond just a mood, is there a symbolism to raking them?
    - o To watching them?
- Describe the falling leaves.
- Describe the bare tree.

Write a road trip poem.

Do you know this road well or is it new to you?
Is this a place you feel as if you belong?
Why are you taking this trip?
What does it mean to be on your way to somewhere else?
Are you going by choice or are you obligated to go?

Imagine that you are a recording device (camera, audio recorder, some not yet designed object that records texture).

- Describe something that you are actually experiencing.
- What about that thing surprises you as you investigate it?
- Is there emotion attached to that surprise?
- Take away words until you believe that you have used the least number of descriptors that will share your experience with a reader.

Related poems:

"On the Road Before Rain" (p. 1), *"Virginia Christmas"* (p. 2), *"Themselves Each One"* (p. 3), *"Airborne"* (p. 5), *"Roseburg"* (p. 16), *"The Intrusion"* (p. 18), *"A Fire if it Burns"* (p. 20), *"Still a Part of that Freedom"* (p. 21), *"My Mother Told Me"* (p. 24), *"Firewood"* (p. 26), *"Above the American"* (p. 29), *"Alone"* (p. 32)

ACKNOWLEDGMENTS

Special thanks goes to my wife Karly for her incomparable love and support over 30 years, and to my son, Steve, for being the finest son a father could ever hope to have.

A special thank you also to Poet Kim Shuck, who served as the 7th Poet Laureate of San Francisco, and who has certainly helped to put these poems and others in the running for publication. I am indebted to her for her kind support and wonderful mentorship.

I would like to thank my Ohlone sister in spirit, Linda Yamane, for her kind support of my poems and for her incredible work in reviving and continuing the historical legacy of Ohlone basket weaving and the Ohlone language; it most certainly would have been lost without her amazing effort.

Thanks to everyone who has helped me through my life, including the best public librarian in America, Sharai Smith; longtime dear poet friend, Patrice Vecchione; and my endorsers and cheerleaders: Deborah Miranda,Tongo Eisen-Martin, Linda Noel, Kitty Costello, Lance Hensen, and Georgina Marie.

Thank you to Heyday Press, including Margaret Dubin and Malcolm Margolin; Poet Laureate of El Dorado County, Lara Gularte; fellow DJ, musician and friend, Mignon Geli; fellow poet and comrade, Lucy Lang Day; and my mentor and friend, the late Lucille Clifton.

My old friends from childhood deserve thanks: Tom Segali, Terry Mosolf, and the late Randy Sinclair. And thank you to **ALL** my Ohlone ancestral family and the pioneers, as well.

Thank you to J. K. Fowler, Laura Salazar, and the friendly folks at Nomadic Press.

Appreciation to my parents, Roy Jr. & Eunice Meadows, who have passed but are still with me in spirit; my Grandparents, the late Roy & Rena Meadows; my late uncle and aunt, Claude & Phyllis Smith; and my parents-in-law, Don & Margaret Showalter.

The following poems have been previously published or are forthcoming in other projects or anthologies:

"We Are Yet Innocent" appeared in the San Francisco Public Library's poem of the day project on 9/10/2020; and

"On the Road Before Rain" will appear in the anthology, *Beat Not Beat*, eds. Rich Fergusson, Alexis Rhone Fancher, and Kim Shuck.

Stephen Meadows

Stephen Meadows is a California poet with roots in both the Ohlone and the pioneer soil of his home state. He was born and raised on the Monterey Bay of Central California and received his secondary education at U.C. Santa Barbara and U.C. Santa Cruz, where he earned his Bachelor of Arts Degree and went on to earn a Master's Degree at San Francisco State University. In addition to writing poetry, Stephen has dedicated over 30 years to public radio as a programmer of folk music from America, Canada, Ireland, and the British Isles, in addition to working more than 20 years as an educator and mentor in the public schools. Meadows is a descendant of native peoples who built the Carmel Mission, gold rush families who settled in the gold country of the foothills and a farm family in Carmel Valley, and his poems are steeped in the indelible aura of California.

COVER MISSIVE

On "Tlu gv"
by Kim Shuck (photographed by Doug Salin)

"Tlu gv" is the result of many years of beading. It's a thing I've been doing for so long my parents don't remember when I started learning. Beads are a very different medium than paint or pencil because it's impossible to physically blend the colors. When I want to create a color I don't have I need to trick the eye. I like to play with texture and surface treatment. This piece was made specifically for the cover of *Winter Work*. I've been living with the poems in this book for over a year and this piece of beading is some of what I have to say about Stephen's poetry. I think that one of the great shifts in my work has happened because I found a photographer that can take an image of what I meant to say. This tree knows a few things and Doug did a great job helping me show that.

Nomadic Press Emergency Fund

Nomadic Press Black Writers Fund

Right before Labor Day 2020 (and in response to the effects of COVID), Nomadic Press launched its Emergency Fund, a forever fund meant to support Nomadic Press-published writers who have no income, are unemployed, don't qualify for unemployment, have no healthcare, or are just generally in need of covering unexpected or impactful expenses.

Funds are first come, first serve, and are available as long as there is money in the account, and there is a dignity centered internal application that interested folks submit. Disbursements are made for any amount up to $300.

All donations made to this fund are kept in a separate account. The Nomadic Press Emergency Fund (NPEF) account and associated processes (like the application) are overseen by Nomadic Press authors and the group meets every month.

On Juneteenth (June 19) 2020, Nomadic Press launched the Nomadic Press Black Writers Fund (NPBWF), a forever fund that will be directly built into the fabric of our organization for as long as Nomadic Press exists and puts additional monies directly into the pockets of our Black writers at the end of each year.

Here is how it works:

$1 of each book sale goes into the fund.

At the end of each year, all Nomadic Press authors have the opportunity to voluntarily donate none, part, or all of their royalties to the fund.

Anyone from our larger communities can donate to the fund. This is where you come in!

At the end of the year, whatever monies are in the fund will be evenly distributed to all Black Nomadic Press authors that have been published by the date of disbursement (mid-to-late December).

The fund (and associated, separate bank account) has an oversight team comprised of four authors (Ayodele Nzinga, Daniel B. Summerhill, Dazié Grego-Sykes, and Odelia Younge) + Nomadic Press Executive Director J. K. Fowler.

Please consider supporting these funds. You can also more generally support Nomadic Press by donating to our general fund via nomadicpress.org/donate and by continuing to buy our books.

As always, thank you for your support!

Scan the QR code for more information and/or to donate.

You can also donate at nomadicpress.org/store.